IRON SCULPTURE

One of the 30.   B 2

BEN-ZION

IRON SCULPTURE

Edited by Lillian Dubin and Tabita Shalem

Alpine Fine Arts Collection Ltd.
New York 1985

Library of Congress Catalog Number: 84–072532

ISBN 0–88168–124–5

First Edition

Contents

Statement by the Artist

I

It is very difficult for an artist in our time to find his way because there are so many strange ways to distract him from his own way. And if an artist gives up his own way — what is left to him? — just to follow the fashion of the time which means the destruction of art and the artist.

All phenomena of life are subject to expression in art and I have allowed myself to follow this belief. Thus the themes and motifs of my creations are diverse — giving free rein to my feelings and impressions. Nature graciously gave me many motifs which I followed and worked on. The Bible revealed itself to me in many of its aspects and also the heritage of my nation with which I feel deep affinity endowed me with insight to its inner life and revealed itself in my work prominently.

All those elements which form the bulk of my work I followed with devotion and tried to find the right materials and ways of expressing them — away from the turmoil and Fata Morganas of the art world. I hope time and places will be gracious to them.

Ben-Zion

Poetic insight and a language of art uniquely his own are characteristic of the work of Ben-Zion. These two elements form the warp and the woof of all his creations bound by an inner necessity and an urgency to communicate. An important element in his creative life is his love for primitive and archaic art and his passion for gathering around him objects and naturalia of all kinds which, he frankly states, are his school for learning about art. Iron sculpture is a milestone in a life of creative output in many media through which the same man speaks. His life and his art are inseparable.

Ben-Zion was born in 1897 in Stary Constantin, Ukraine. His father, Hirsh Weinman, a cantor, emigrated to Tarnopol where he served as chazan in the main synagogue until 1909, and then to Tarnov where he was cantor in the largest synagogue in Galicia.

As a boy Ben-Zion studied in a yeshiva and with private teachers. He began to write poetry in Hebrew and showed an inclination to draw pictures, activities which his father discouraged. During the First World War, while living in Vienna as a refugee, he tried to attend the Art Academy, but was hindered by the anti-Semitic attitude toward East European Jews and gave up this endeavor. In 1918, after the Russians evacuated Galicia, his family returned to a devastated Tarnov. Following the death of Ben-Zion's father in 1920, the family emigrated to America to start a new life.

Drawing by Ben-Zion when he was a young boy, of his father.

II

In 1921 Ben-Zion joined a group of Hebrew writers in New York, the first Hebrew poets on American soil, and together with this group (among whom were the outstanding poets Bavli, Halkin, and Silkiner) published his first drama, poems, and fairy tales in Hebrew. He supported himself at this time by giving private lessons. Hebrew was not popular in America in those days and those who wrote in this language felt disappointed over the inadequate demand for their work. Finding themselves almost entirely without a reading public, they felt that the soil was not fertile for anyone writing in Hebrew. Were it not for their teaching positions in various institutions, most of them couldn't have persevered in their work. Ben-Zion could not adjust himself to teaching in a Hebrew institution—his struggle went on until 1933 when Nazism and all its horrors started in Germany. He felt that language was a helpless vehicle for expression in such times for evil-doers used the same idealistic words for their destructive deeds as those who opposed oppression. Literary writing seemed to him like empty phraseology, like a scream that nobody hears. He felt so too about his own work, and could no longer continue to write.

Looking for a new medium of expression through which he could create his own language, he turned again to his dream of drawing and painting. And thus his new career started—hesitatingly, almost subconsciously.

In 1936 Ben-Zion had his first one-man show at the Artist's Gallery. Together with a group of young artists who shared the same struggle to create something new in art, a group called "The Ten" was formed. Over the years, artists such as Rothko, Gottlieb, and others emerged as non-objective painters while Ben-Zion continued in his own way—representational expression based on the abstract. With time the rift widened, and the group disbanded.

Curt Valentin was drawn to the work of this artist and first exhibited at his Buchholz Gallery a cycle of pen and ink drawings titled "The Weather Vane"—an imaginative rendering of the aimless turning of a weather vane with the winds of our time. Valentin later published three portfolios of his Biblical etchings—part of a series of four. The third portfolio "Job, Ruth, Song of Songs" was Valentin's last publication. He died in Italy in 1950. It was not until 1962 that the fourth portfolio "Judges and Kings" was published by Graphophile in keeping with the design of the first three volumes. The strong sculptural feeling in Ben-Zion's painting and etching seem to lead inevitably to his work in iron sculpture.

Ben-Zion started to do iron sculpture about the year 1959 long after he had established a reputation as a painter. It happened naturally as it does with every medium in which he expresses himself. From early childhood wood, rocks, metals, and minerals of all kinds have fascinated him and have been his playthings at all stages of his life. His gathering of pebbles are an invariable part of any walks or excursions he has ever taken and his drawings on their surfaces are as countless in number as the pebbles he has gathered from the shores of the sea, streams, brooks and rivers, and from the meadows, fields, and woods he loves to explore.

III

THE STONE IN THE FIELD

The stone in the field is not
 alone or abandoned.
Securely it lies in the embrace
 of the earth
Like a child in the lap
 of its mother.

And if there is a disturbance in
 the tranquility of its repose
It secures itself to the body
 of the earth
Closely, closely, until they are
 as one
And there is no more disturbance
 between them.

The birth of the stone happens
 slowly, slowly
In harmony with all the elements.
None of the elements will hasten
 or retard,
Everything in the right season
 will develop.

The stone in the field is not alone—
It lies securely in the cradle of creation.
It becomes form and changes form
From every side that we look at it.
It enriches and fertilizes our imagination
And helps the artist in creating
 his creations.

From SONGS OF BEN-ZION II
Translated from the Hebrew

Ben-Zion is very much drawn to masks—especially those from primitive cultures. They are all around him in his home—masks from different parts of the world and those of his own creation from wood, stone, shell, and iron—mingling freely with one another. The earliest masks he made were from wood and many of them were inspired by the beauty of the driftwood he gathered one summer on Sutton Island in Maine.

IV

Ben-Zion's collecting is one of the three passions that go back to his earliest days in Galicia. The other two are art and poetry. As a boy he used to bring home bent nails, broken horseshoes and other treasures, hiding them under the piano away from the eyes of his disapproving mother. But these first collections never really had a chance to accumulate, for every spring Ben-Zion's mother would discard his precious objects as part of her pre-Passover cleaning and he would have to start all over again. And he always did.

Iron is the material Ben-Zion chose to do the main body of his work in sculpture. From his love and caring for iron throughout his life he has grown to know it in a most intimate way. It lends itself admirably to his strong sense for abstract design; his subjects evolve in a form that is unmistakably his own. In none of his works is there a tendency to copy nature, yet as in primitive art to which he closely relates, through the design he achieves a strong relationship to the subject rendered.

Ben-Zion's themes are manifold. As he has himself pointed out, the finding of the iron and the surroundings in which the material was worked have often influenced the theme of the sculpture. Many pieces express his sheer delight with the materials. They play together like melodies, as in his "Twenty Variations on a Theme."

Some of the large pieces of sculpture are on insect motifs—Wasp, Praying Mantis, etc. In them the airy lightness and fragile form of the insects take on a monumentality, and the heaviness of the iron becomes light and delicate.

Birds of all kinds are like a thread through all the tapestry of the iron works of Ben-Zion. In the 1930's when his early paintings appeared, one of his major opuses at that time was a canvas titled "Iron Bird," perhaps a premonition of iron birds to appear more than a quarter of a century later. The rooster, a favorite subject in his paintings, takes on another dimension in the sculpture. The farm implements that went into their construction are sublimated and preserve in their ironness both the handiwork of a time past and the virile quality of the living creature. In common with the birds, animals of all kinds from the land and sea emerge in Ben-Zion's work—each with his own marked characteristic, and often with a playfulness and humor.

Ben-Zion's lifetime study of the Bible, his affinity for world literature and the antique world are expressed in his paintings and in his iron sculpture. Gilgamesh, Don Quixote, the Prophets, the Patriarchs, and especially Moses, people his world of creation. They mirror the search for an answer to man's perplexities from the beginning of time.

There is nothing arbitrary in the work of Ben-Zion. Whatever he creates is uncontrived, in keeping with his character and his strong feeling for the subject. Form is reduced to its essentials and emanates the poetic simplicity of a beginning creation. There is no attempt made to impress the spectator with craft or technique. It is the vision of the poet-artist on the little traveled road that those who seek must reach out to find.

Iron Sculpture

1. This Was a Shovel, Now It Is a Mask   10½″

*2 Praying Prophet   12″

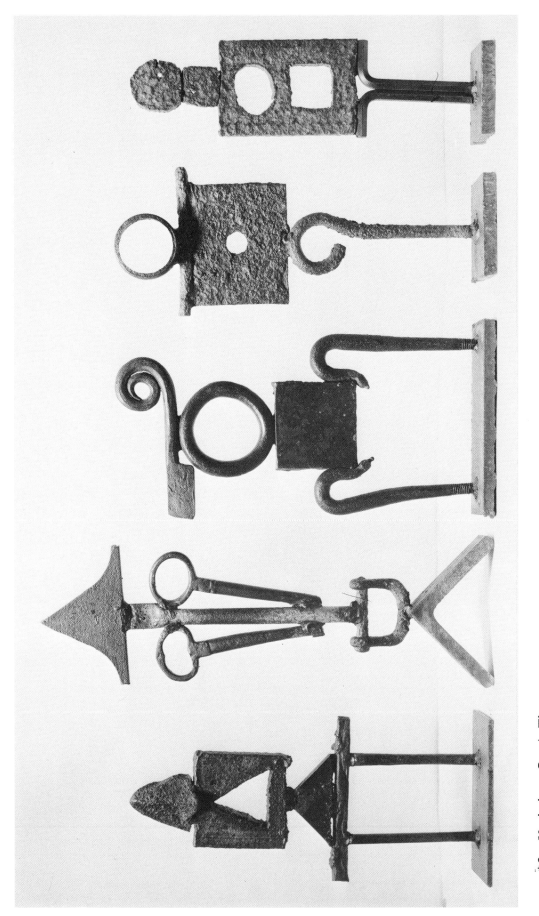

*3. Variations On A Theme

a. 14"   b. 17"   c. 14½"   d. 14"   e. 13½"

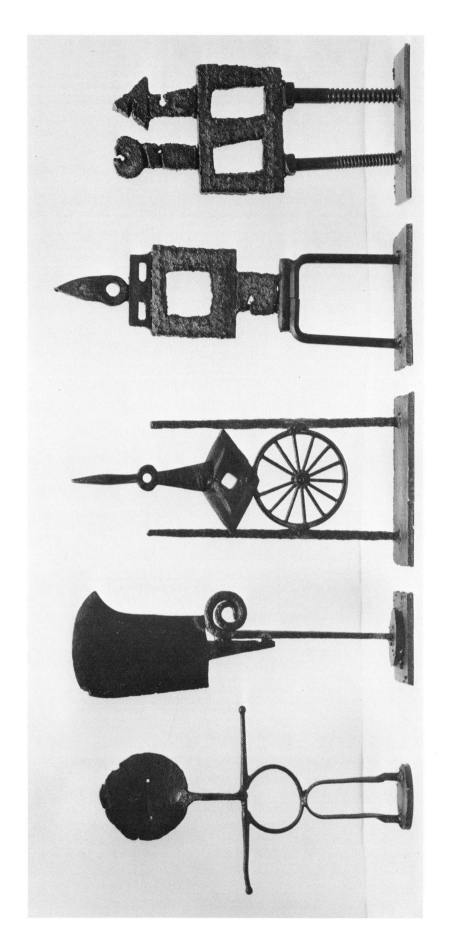

4. Variations On A Theme

f. 12½"   g. 14"   h. 14"   i. 13"   j. 12"

5. Variations On A Theme

o. 26"

n. 19"

m. 27"

l. 16"

k. 23"

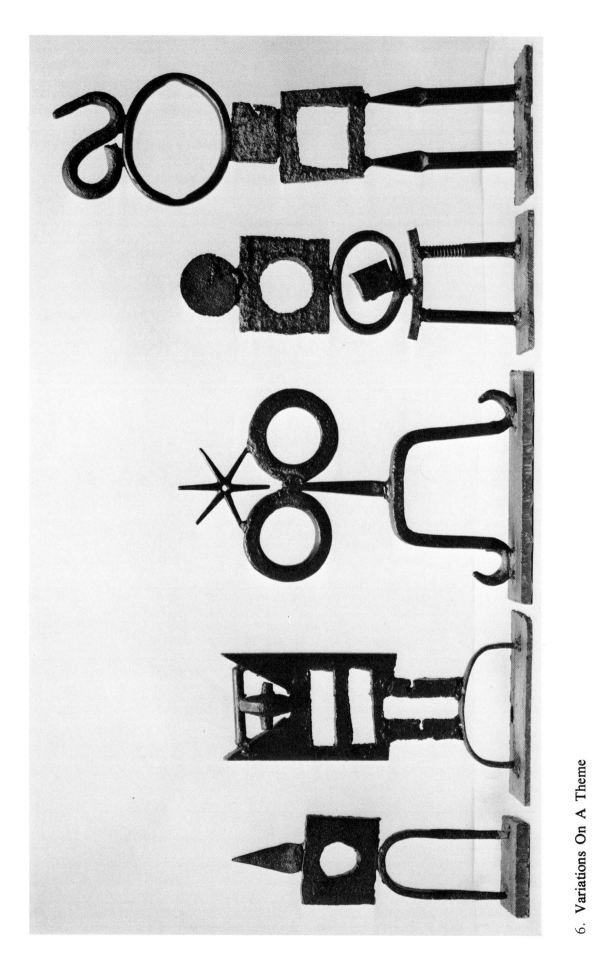

6. **Variations On A Theme**

p. 11½"   q.12"   r. 14"   s. 14"   t. 18"

*7 Old Indian Head   52″

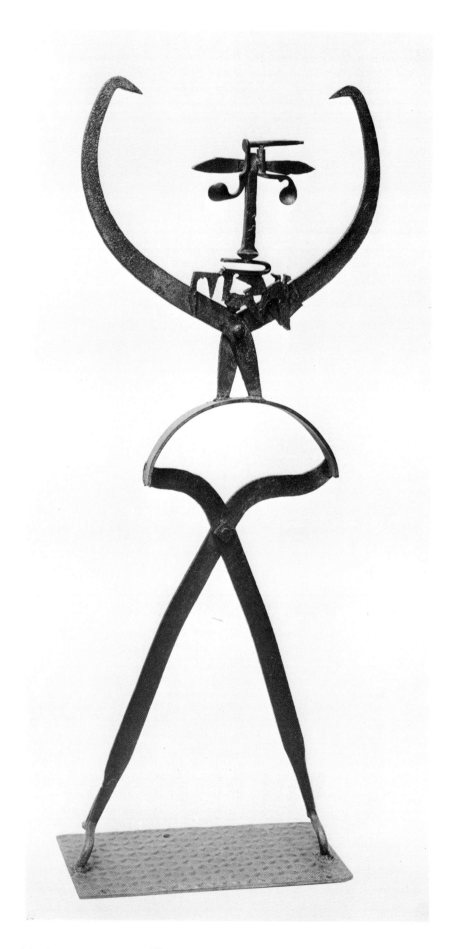

*8 Greek Dancer   50″

9. Centaur 29½"

*10. Caterpillar   16″

11. Wild Beast   23″

12. Mechanical Tools

a. 9"

b. 11"

13. Acrobat   28″

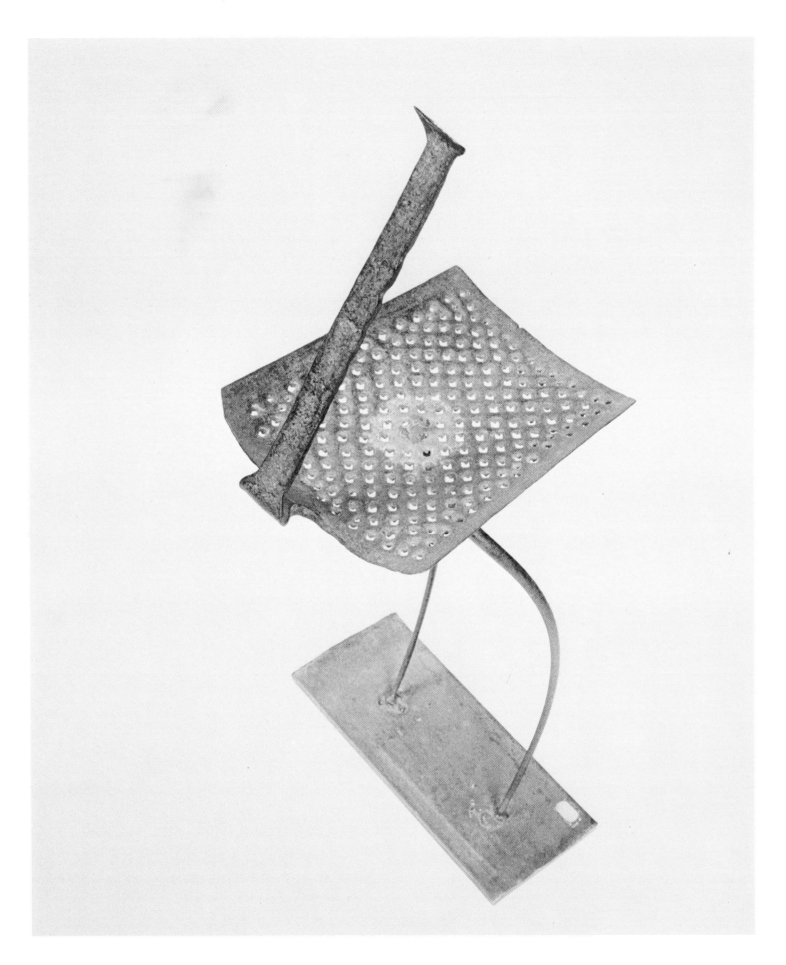

14. Ostrich 24"

Prehistoric Skeleton   10"

15. German Mythical Figure   10"

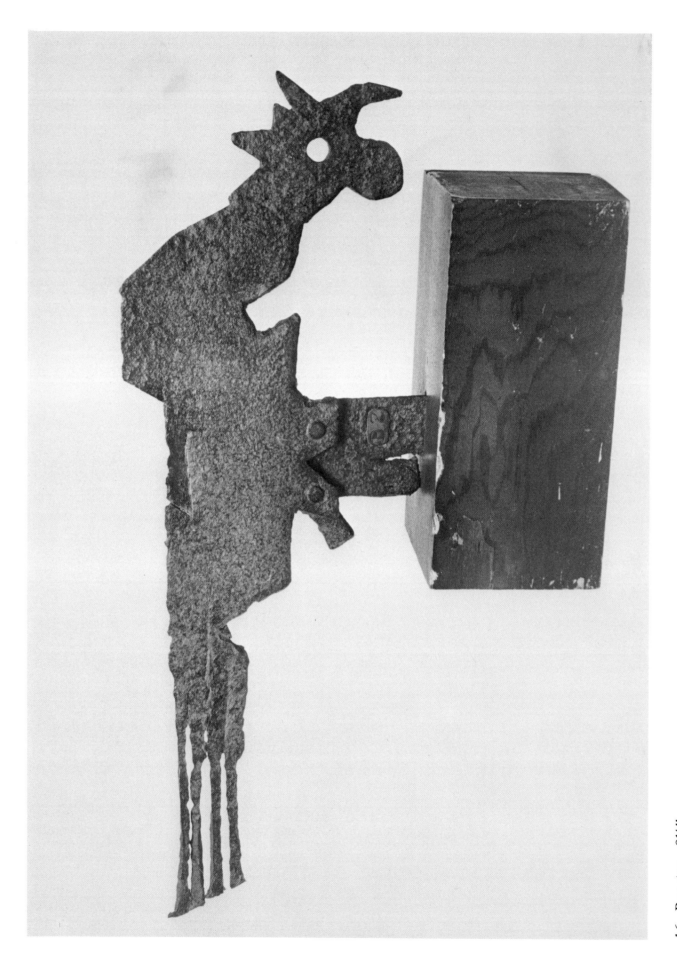

16. Rooster 9½"

17. Fighting Warriors 7″

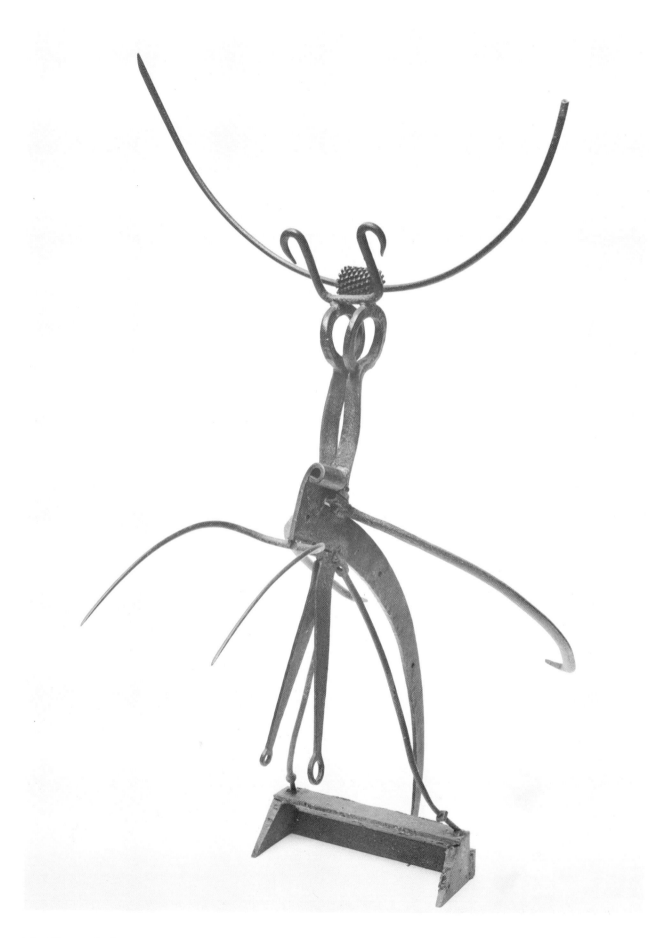

18. Wasp   35″

19. Owl   6½″

19. Angel   8½″

19. Bird Looking Back   8″

20. Weasel 6½″

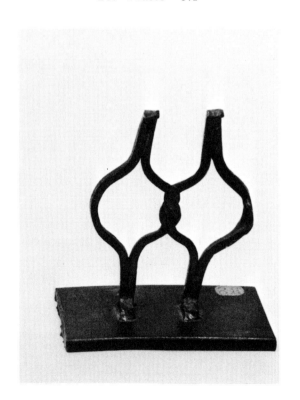

20. Twins 6″

20. Man With Raised Arms 8½″

21. Figure II   10½″

21. African Bird   10″

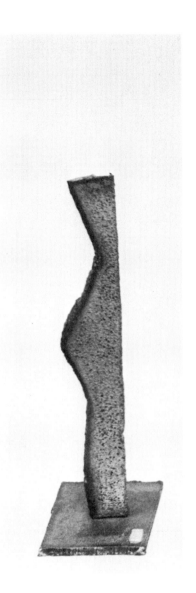

21. Figure I   9″

*22. Beast 13"

23. Mechanical Head   14″

24. Owl 9″

24. Dancer 11½″

24. Figure 8¾″

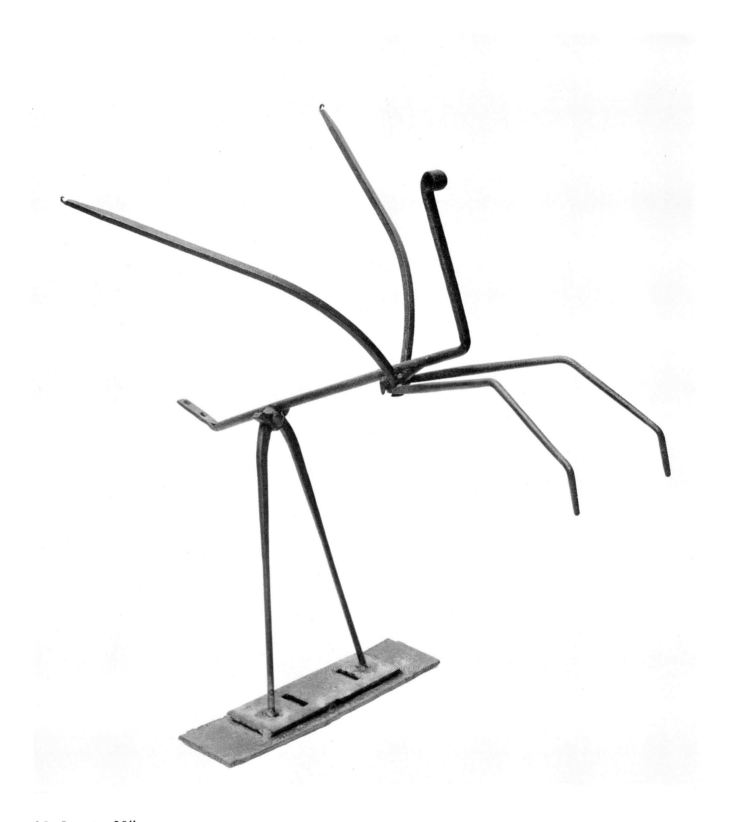

25. Insect 28"

26. Crowing Rooster   27"

*27. Cow   9″

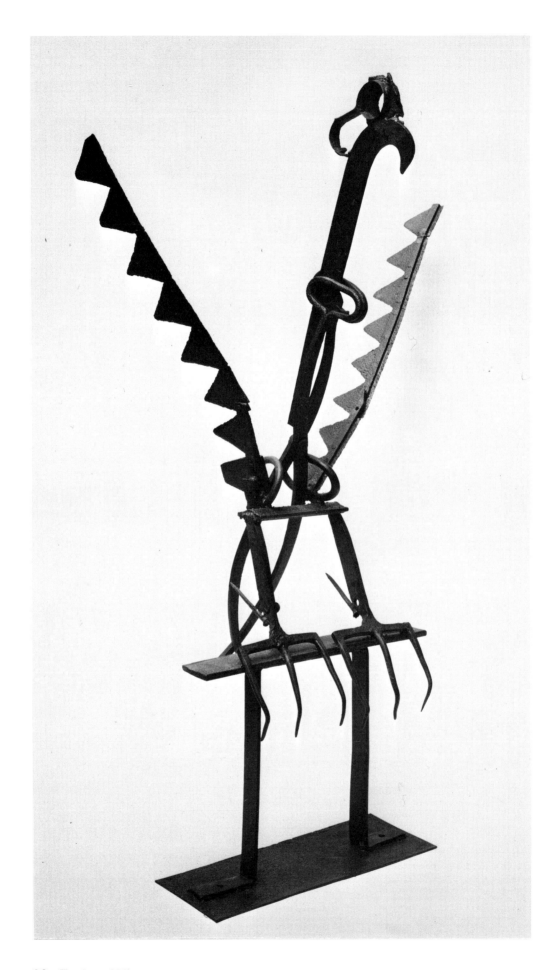

28. Eagle   49″

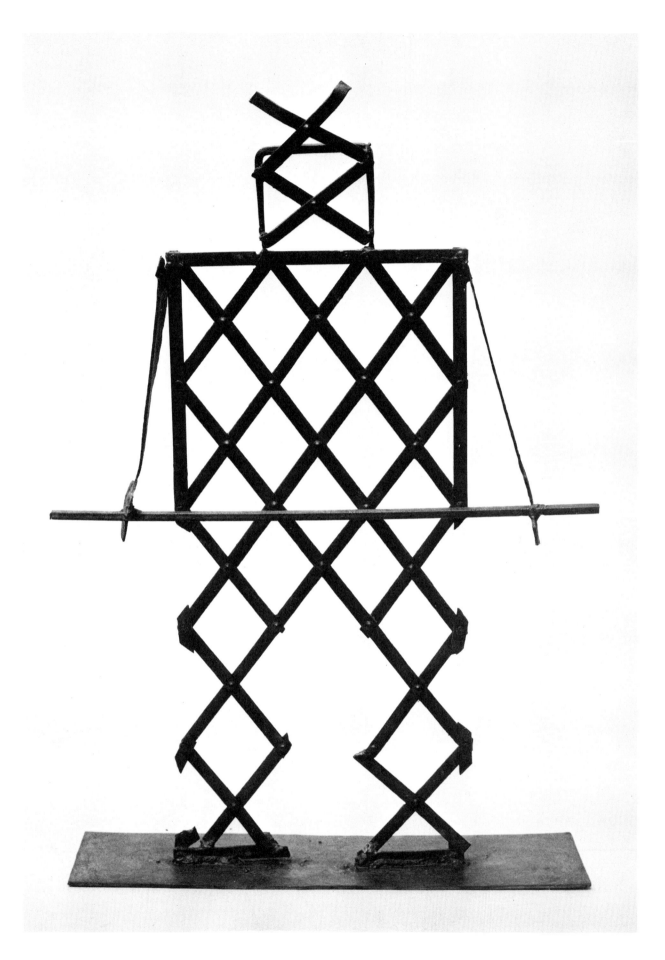

29. Circus Manager 23½″

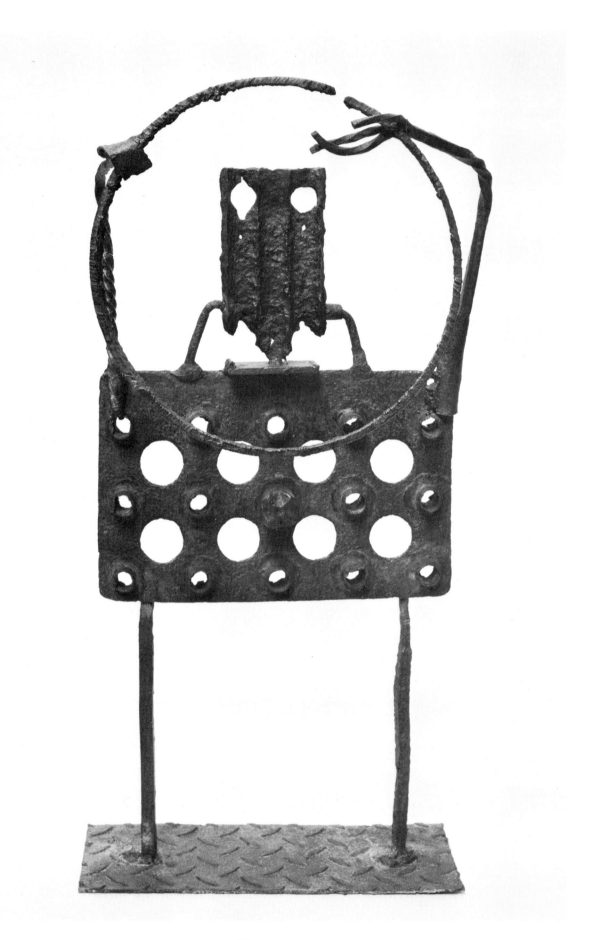

*30. Man A Victim Of His Own Devices   39″

31. Rooster On A Fence   19"

*32. Masks

a. 12" b. 11" c. 14" d. 13½" e. 17" f. 12½"

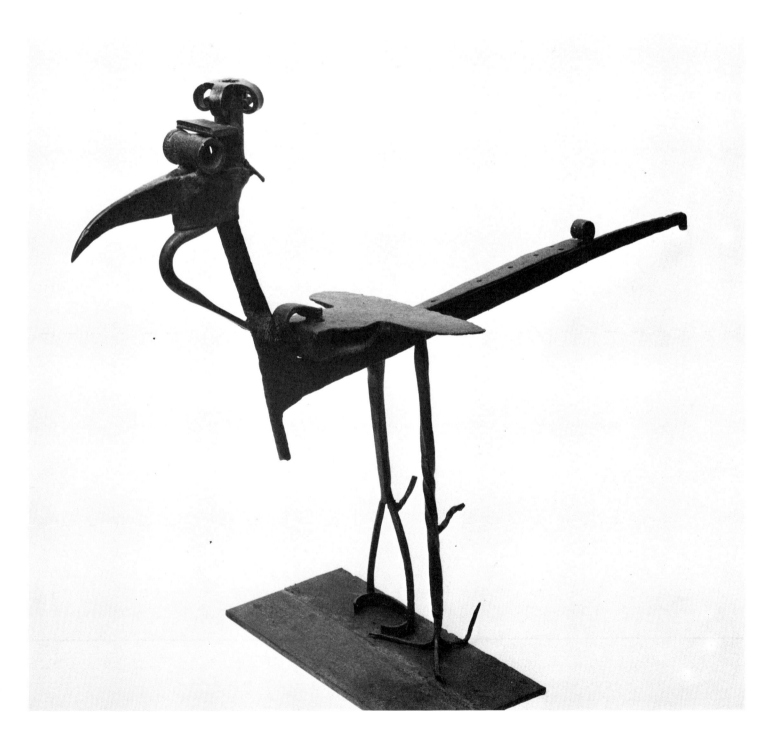

*33. Strange Bird   32½″

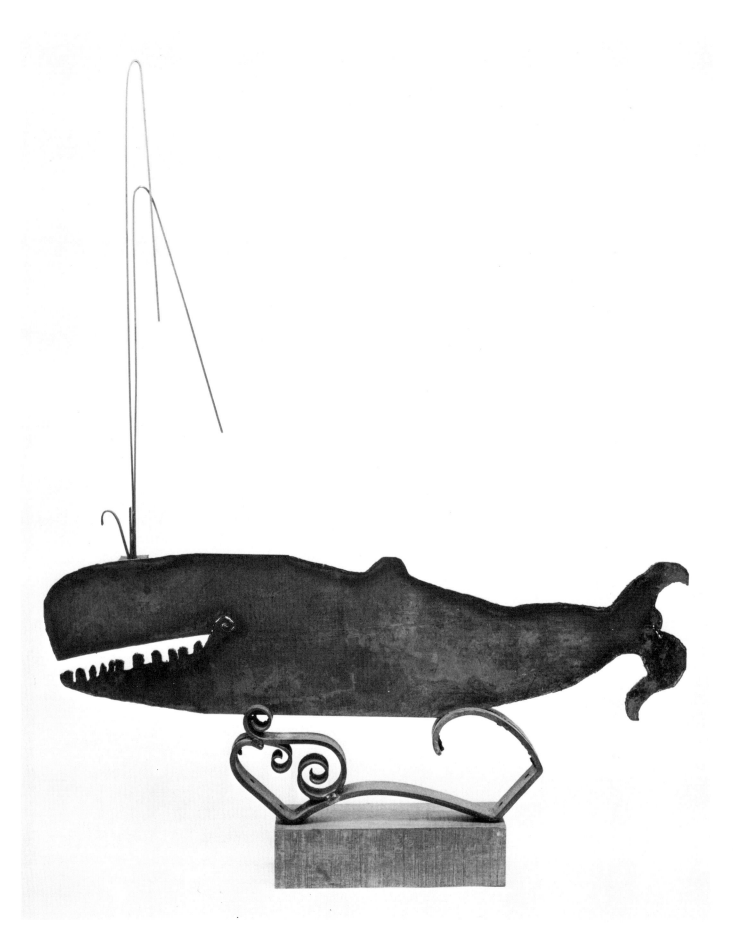

34. Whale   18″

35. Praying Man   28½″

36. Moses And The Falling Tablets   27″

*37. Enkidu 17½"

38. Don Quixote 12″

39. Praying Mantis I   18″

40. Abstract Figure   13½″

41 Poet Laureatus II 18"

*41. Poet Laureatus I 20"

42. Praying Mantis II   62"

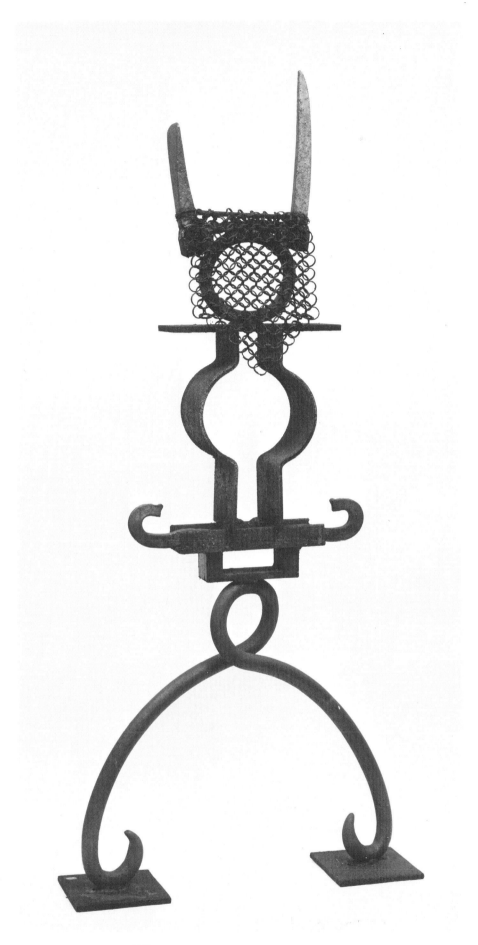

43. Minotaur   51½″

44. Sacrifice Of Isaac   54"

*45. Jacob's Dream   46″

a. 6½″

b. 11½″

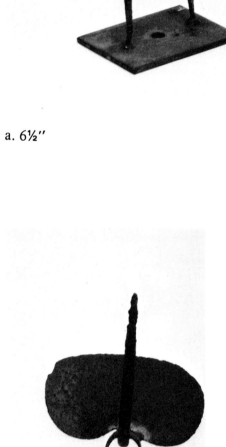

c. 11½″

d. 8″

46. Strange Birds

e. 3¾″

f. 4½″

g. 4½″

47. Strange Birds

48. Eagle On Its Nest   20½″

49. Figure   13½″

*50. Moses   25″

51. Head Of A Giant Bird   9″

a. 9″

b. 10″

c. 8½″

52. Masks

a. 8″

53. Masks

b. 13″

54. Circus   24″

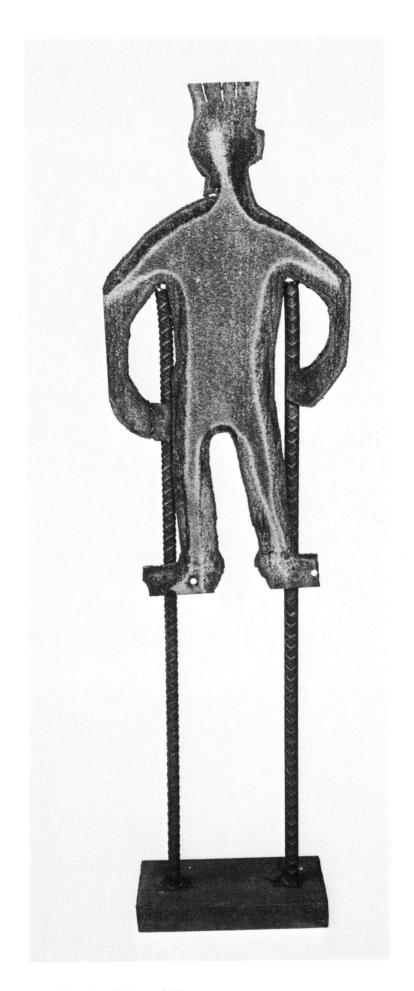

55. Man On Stilts   48″

56. Bathers In A Private Pool   4½"

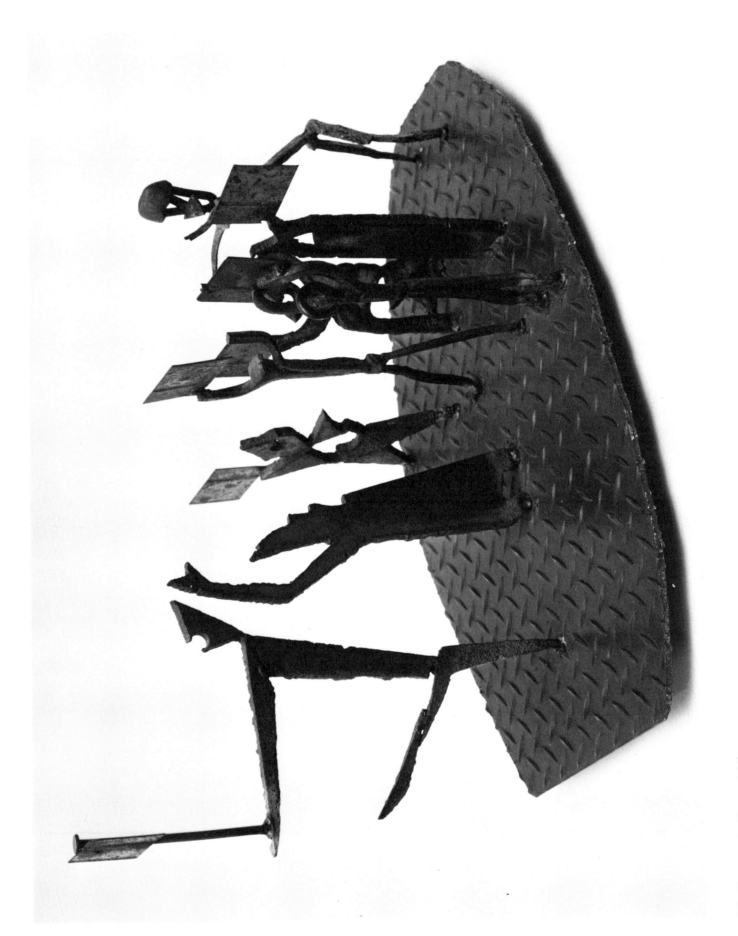

57. Demonstration 18"

a. 7″

b. 14½″

c. 14½″

58. Masks

59. Father and Son   13"

Bird   10″

Little Figure   6″

Little Woman   6″

Owl   12″

Deer   5½″   Ostrich   9″

60.

61. Bird On My Spiral Staircase   17½"

62. Colosseum   8″

63. Perplexed Bird   20"

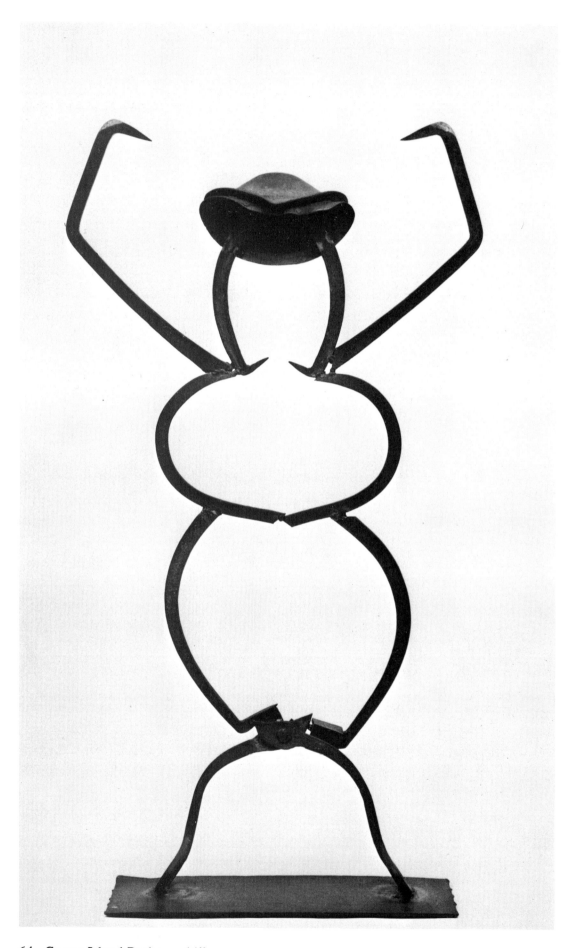

64. Coney Island Bather   44″

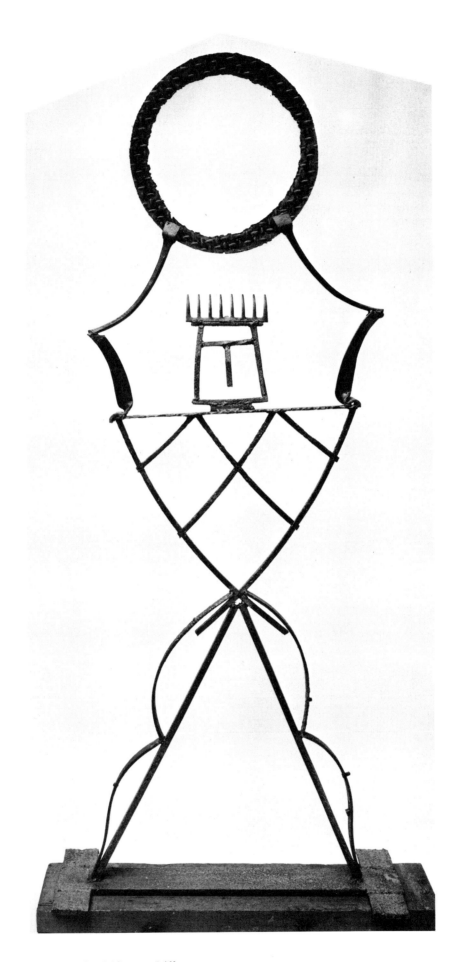

65. Weight Lifter   54″

a. 9″

b. 9″

66. Iron Masks

c. 12″

67. Fish 9"

68. Bull   19"

69. Young Girl   29"

*70. Mother and Child   14″

*70. Woman Washing Hair   13″

71. Bird Through A Window   8″

71. Bird Looking Back   8½″

71.   Warrior   13½″

71. Bird With Long Beak   8½″

72. Woman Riding Horse Side Saddle   8½″

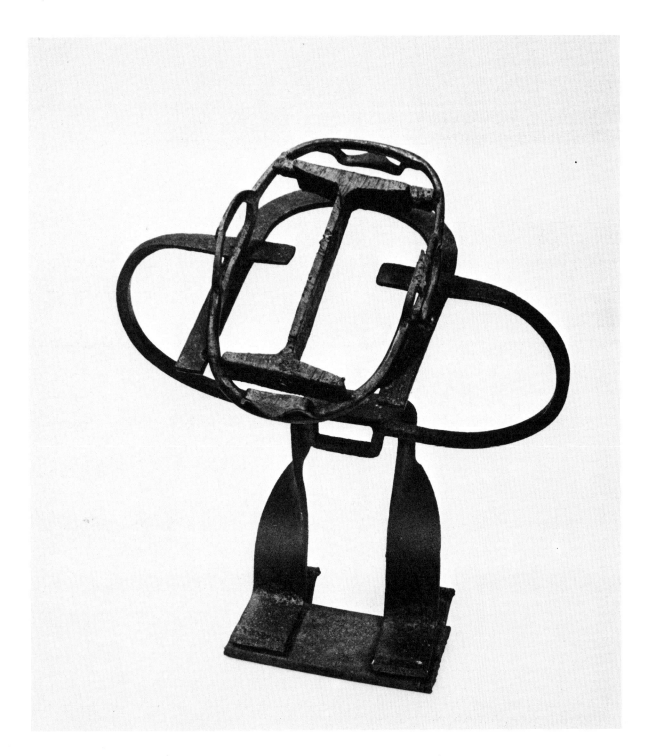

73. Ball Player   17″

74. Incarcerated   31"

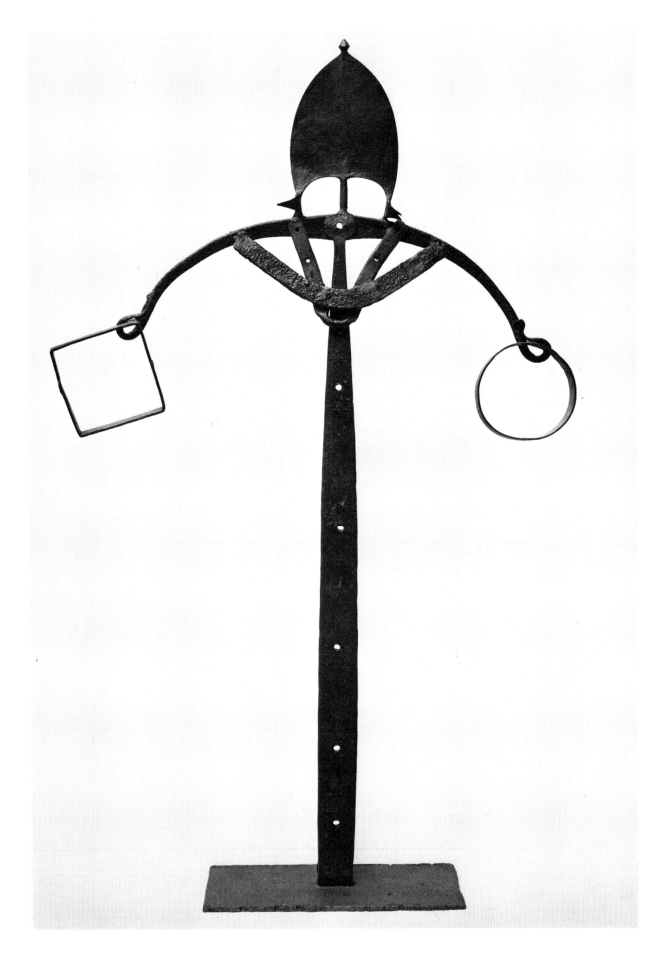

75. Bishop   54″

*76. Moses Writing The Tablets   24″

77. Moses On Top Of The Mountain 30″

78. Moses Carrying The Tablets   26½″

79. Moses Dropping The Tablets   26½″

80. Moses Sees What Happened Below   28″

81. Moses And The Dropping Tablets   28″

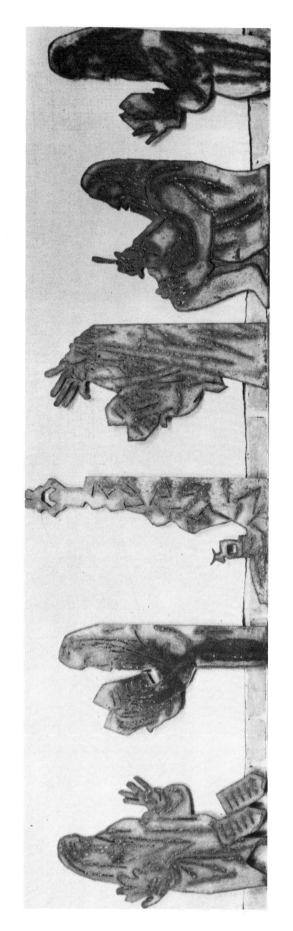

81a. The Moses Group

82. David Playing On The Harp   24″

83. Little Sea Monster   16″

84. Peasant And His Wife   10″

*85. Alighting Eagle   17″

86. African King   15″

87. Quarreling Birds   5″

88. Ruins Of A Temple   7″

* 89. Apocalypse 12"

90. Moses And The Tablets   20″

91. Kohen Blessing Of The Priests

92. Little Kneeling Figure 4½″

92. Female Figure 5″

92. Little Lamb 4″

93. Antique Figure   23″

94. Exotic Bird   11½″

94. Confronting Bird   10½″

94.   Acrobat   27″

95. Greek Sketch   11"

96. Mask From An Old Forest   12½″

97. Figure   8″

98. Arguing Prophet   17½″

99. Ancient Tyrant   13½″

100. Warrior   16″

101. Giant Bird   22″

102. Canaanite Figures   16″

103. Peaceful Birds   17"

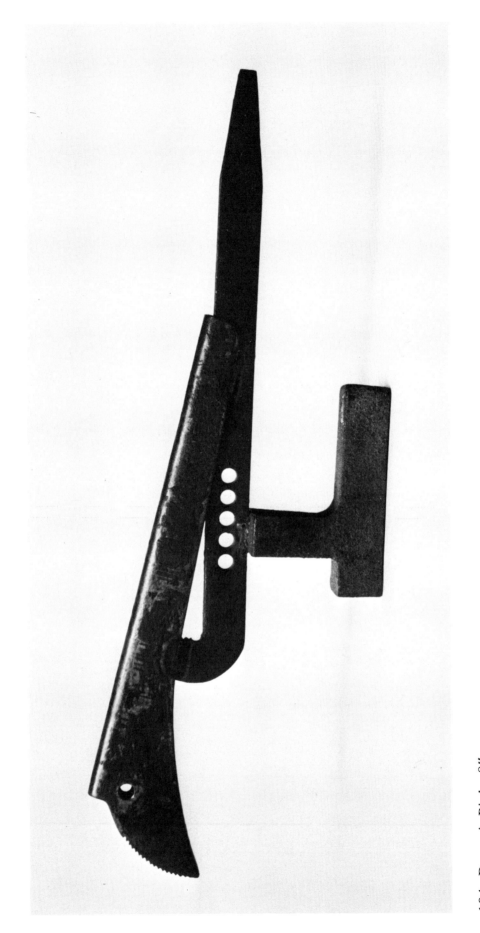

104. Dynamic Bird   8"

105. Bird Preparing For Flight   12½"

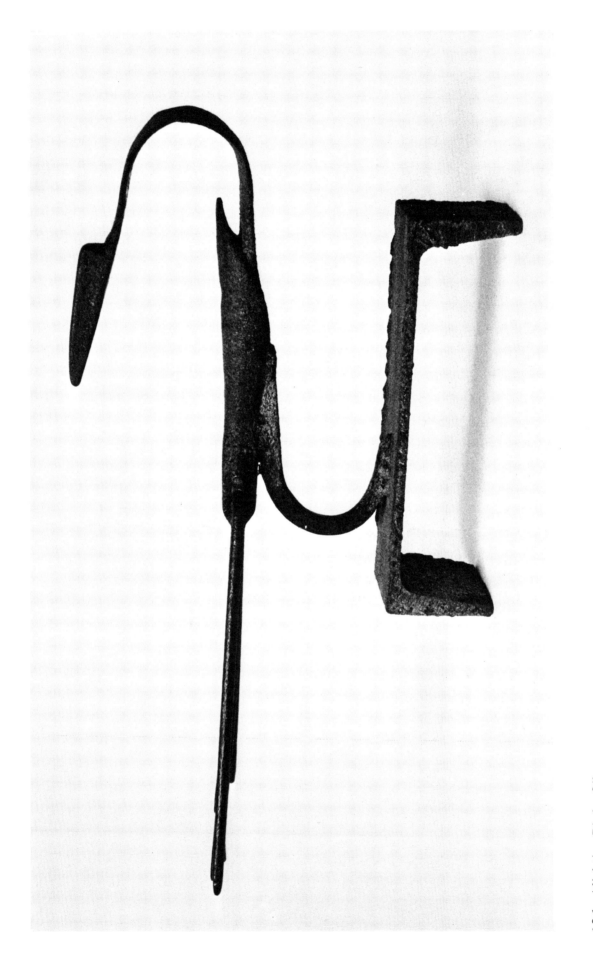

106. Alighting Bird   9"

107. Bird In Flight   12"

108. Diving Bird   13½″

a. Bird Looking Back 5″

b. Roman Figure 4″

c. Little Calf 3″

109.

110. Rooster 24"

a. Strutting Bird   3"

b. Mexican Woman And Child   3"

c. Little Animal   2½"

111.

112. Weasel　8″

113. Figure 14"

113. Child With Balloon 19"

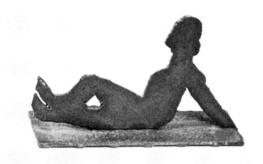

114. Reclining Figure   4½″

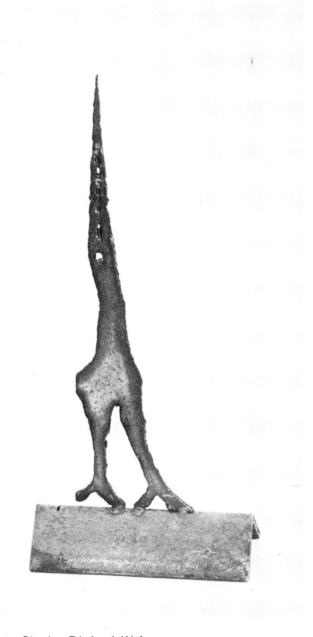

114. Preacher   13″

114. Singing Bird   14½″

115. Pure Design   12¾″

116. Sea Monster   27″

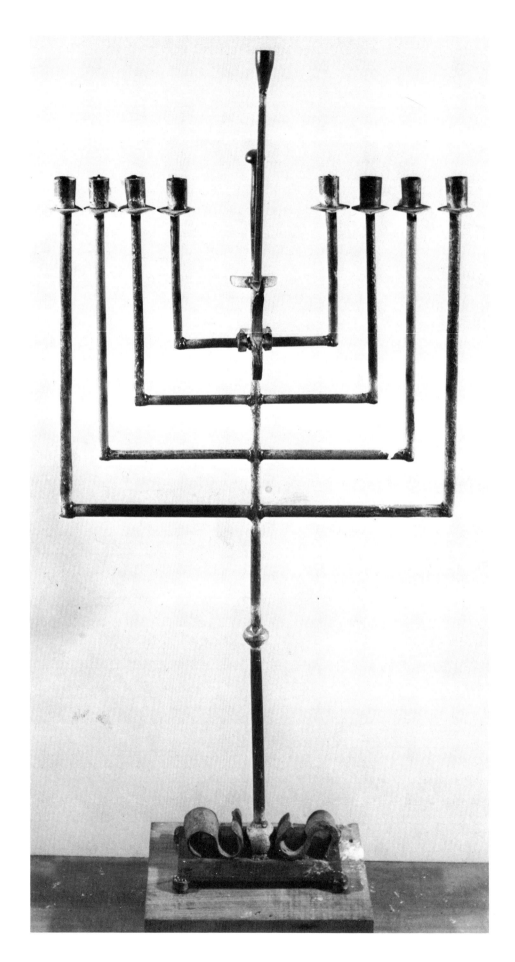

117. Chanukah Menorah   43″

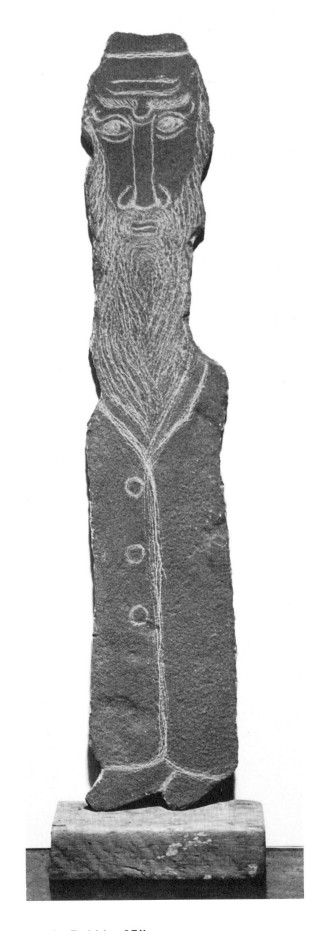

*118. Rabbi   37"

119. Primitive Head   9″

120. Torso   4″

121. The Chief 11½″

122. Emerging Bud   17"

123. Rolling Horse 6½"

124. Blessing Hands   7½"

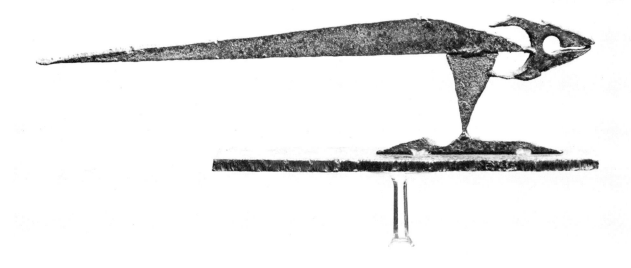

125. Fish Skeleton 6″

126. Bull 15″

*127. A Legend, A Man Buys A House I   a. 24″ b. 9″ c. 9½″ d. 17″

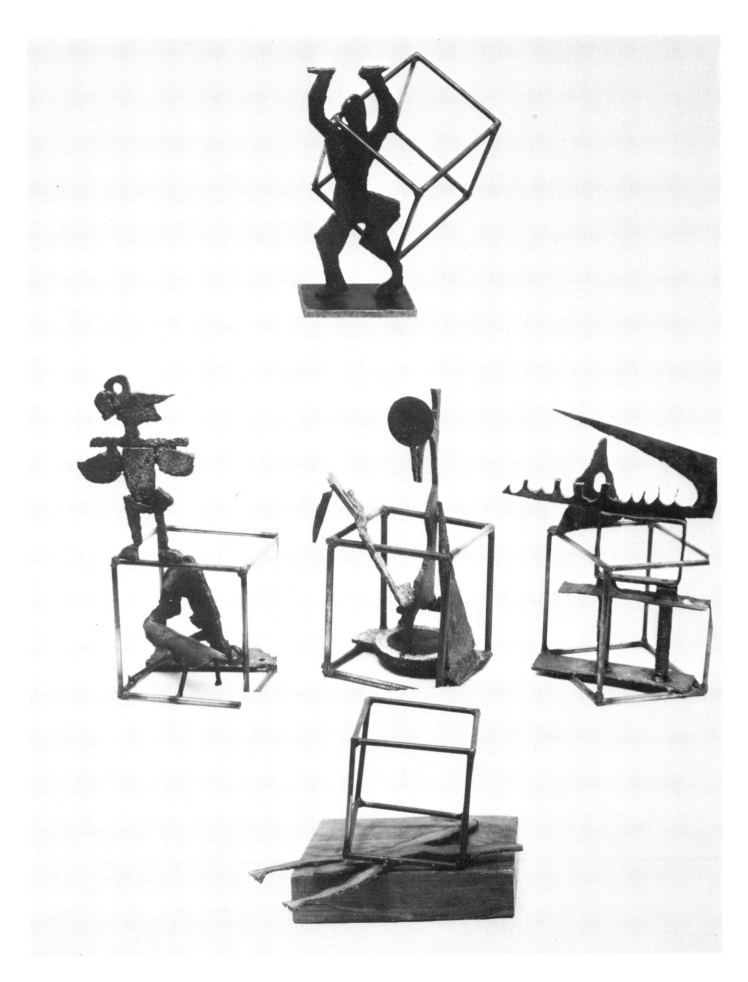

*128. A Legend, A Man Buys A House II   a. 13″ b. 15″ c. 13″ d. 8″

129. Old Age   18″

130. Man In Pursuit Of Success   35″

131. Mexican Head　16½"

*132. Giant Owl   27½″

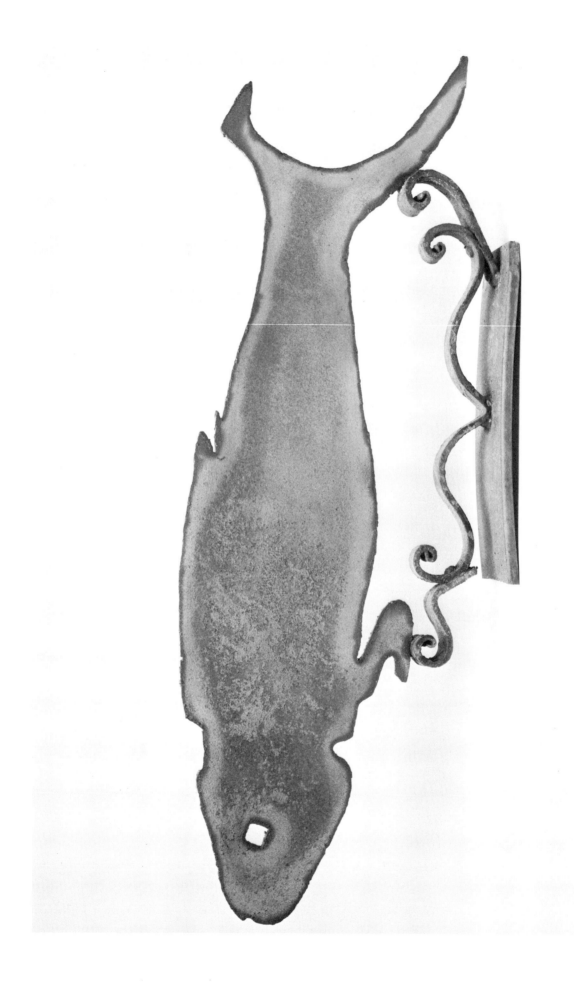

133. Fish And Waves   12½"

*134. Japanese Dancers   28½″, 39″

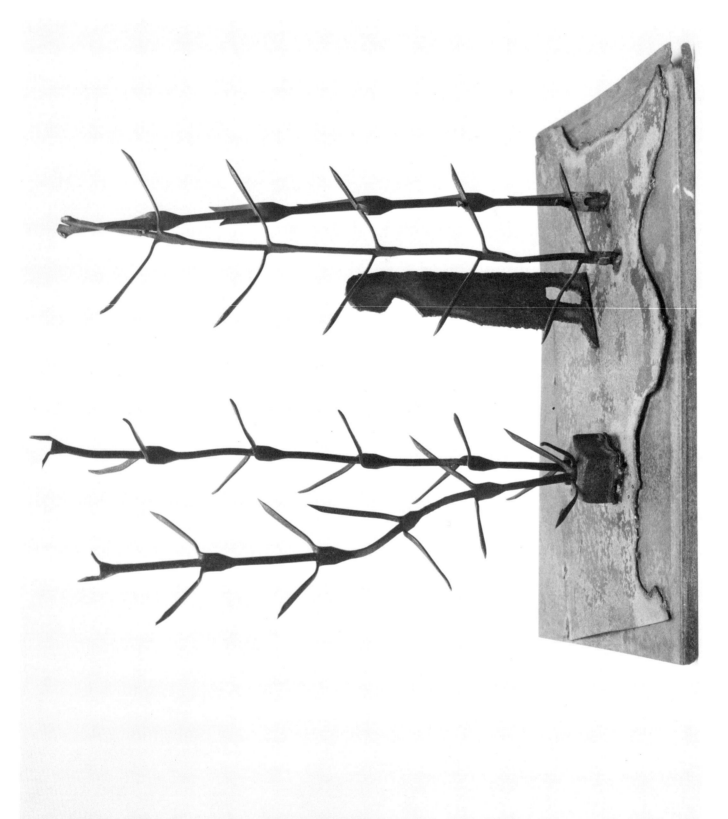

135. Girl In The Woods 21"

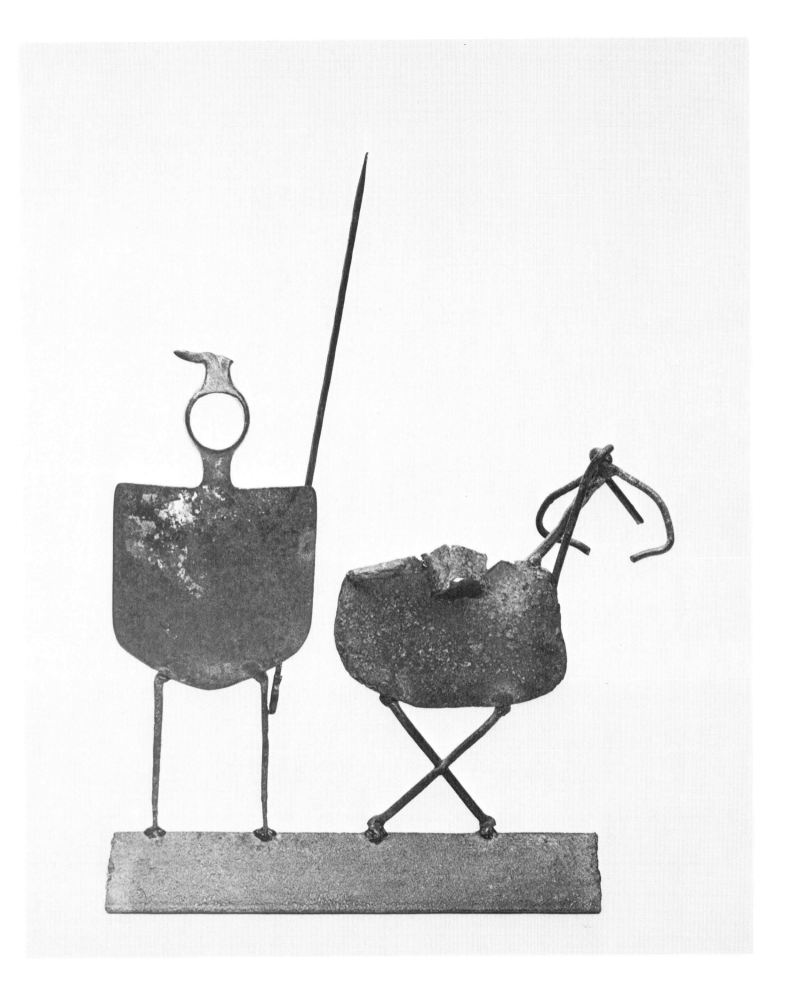

*136. Don Quixote And Sancho Panza   19"

137. Dancer   12″

138. Bird Feeding   6½″

139. Cow 5½"

140. Bird In The Window   7″

141. Chinese Lady   7½″

142. Lizard 6½″

*143. Celestial Sphere   11½″

*144. Celestial Face   8″

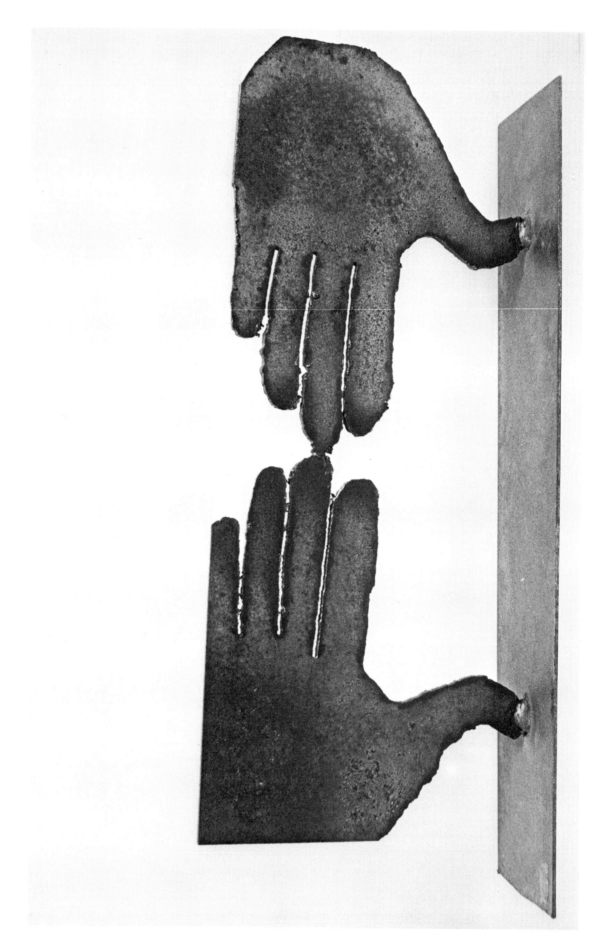

145. Hand Game 7"

146. The End Of The Play, The Actors Bow   5½"

No. 2
Praying
Prophet

One day, that was in 1959, I saw through my window an iron worker cutting iron with a torch like cutting cheese with a knife. This instigated me to make a drawing on a piece of iron that I had in my studio. I took it down to the iron worker, telling him, "I see that you can cut iron with your torch so easily. Could you cut for me this piece of iron according to the lines on it?" "Sure I can", he said. So I told him, "Do it please and I'll give you as much as you ask for it". He took the piece of iron, looked at my chalk drawing, put it on his anvil and started to cut. Within a few minutes the iron became a praying prophet, and this is it, my first piece of iron work. Thus, when I had already my retrospective show at the Jewish Museum, and Curt Valentin had published three volumes of my Biblical etchings, I was inspired by iron to such an extent that it became a major part of my art work.

Nos. 3,4,5,6
Variations

During the time of my retrospective exhibition at the Jewish Museum in 1959 a number of masks in all kinds of materials were included. The New York Times, in the Sunday Magazine Section took special notice of those few masks, reproduced them on a full page and called them "Fanciful Faces".

The name "Fanciful Faces" rather interested me and when I decided to include iron as one of my mediums, those fanciful faces kept on growing on me constantly until they developed their own way of expression. I felt very happy with the iron pieces of my new medium for in order to create a theme, any kind of theme in iron, you have to find the right kind of iron. You can't go into a store and buy so many pounds and pounds of iron of a certain measurement and take it home and work on it. First of all, with modern iron, you don't even know if it is iron. Metallurgical inventions made iron a real bastard of all kinds of metals. And I hated all those different kinds of metals because you really can't tell what they are, especially cast iron. I had to rely on finding old pieces of iron near old houses, abandoned iron works and antique shops where I still could find things made in olden times.

My aim was to work only with old iron and not on all kinds of amalgams. So the one who is constantly hunting for his materials has a good time actually looking for them — finding all kinds of surprises and suggestions. By their nature, one group of the iron pieces I made are distinguished by their resemblance to one another, as if they would be on one theme. When I put them together they harmonized so perfectly that they became a natural group — a variation on a theme. This group of work I created almost as a unit by itself although from time to time I added a number of related pieces of abstract designs which appealed to me like musical abstractions of sounds.

No. 7
Old Indian
Head

A friend of mine rented a house in Santa Fe for the summer. It was an old place with an accumulation in the surrounding area of many old things. That trash pile, as usual, was very interesting to me. The things accumulated were just trash to those who disposed of them. None of those pieces that I picked up showed any effort by the depositors to form them in any way. They were just left-over pieces of metal, also pieces of iron cut according to their needs and discarded after using the necessary parts while building something. I picked up a few of those inspiring pieces that must have been lying there for a long time and got very rusty and bent. One of the pieces I picked up had a marvelous patina of rust and an inspiring reminder of an old face. Because I found it in a place where Indians lived and still live I was instigated, after finishing my work on it, to call it "Old Indian Head".

No. 8
Greek Dancer

Greek Dancer was inspired by a number of different pieces of iron. The mask of it which I composed from suggestive parts reminded me of old Hellenic types.

No. 10
Caterpillar

This is an early American piece which I found in a country store. It was a device which was put on the belly of a cow to wean the calf from her mother. This device is very supple and keeps on moving like a caterpillar which scares the little calf while trying to reach the udder of the cow.

No. 22
Beast

This was supposed to be just a mask but when I came to the completion of the piece a neighbor's child saw it and called out, "This is a beast!" And so it is.

No. 27
Cow

Two horns on a plain piece of iron connected to another piece of iron with two round rings will right away suggest some living animal, and it doesn't have to wait long until it becomes what it really is. And what it is really I really don't have to tell you.

No. 30
Man a Victim
of His Own
Devices

I visited Cripple Creek and its surroundings in Colorado twice. Reading about its gold mines and the big finds and the quick growing of the richness of the vicinity — having even an opera house and big hotels at the turn of the century — also about the way Cripple Creek and neighboring vicinities lost all their fabulous gains until finally they became ghost towns — I saw how quickly they dwindled and all that fantastic development became a nest of ghost towns. It became like a symbol of man's up and down life. There I found very interesting pieces of iron which I used in my work. Imbued with the influence of the quick rise and downfall of that place and its vicinity I made a number of sculptures from the iron and one especially, "Man a Victim of His Own Devices", actually symbolizes Cripple Creek.

No. 32
Masks
a,b,c,d,e,f

The most simple things in a mask are the two holes of the eyes, the elongated or shortened form of the nose, and the appropriate mouth. There is no expression of any kind that exists that cannot be attained within those few limited forms.

No. 33

Strange Bird

The theme of an iron bird occurred in my early paintings many years before I started to work in sculpture.

V

No. 37
Enkidu

The Sumerian epic of Gilgamesh has fascinated me since my youth, and in 1975 I published a portfolio of 36 etchings based on this great work.

No. 41
Poet
Laureatus I, II

Humor is a healthy thing if it is expressed within its limits.

No. 45
Jacob's
Dream

Jacob's Dream is a biblical theme that is recurrent in my work. Here it is in one of my early paintings.

VI

No. 50
Moses

The Moses theme started to interest me when I began to work on my four volumes of etchings of the Pentateuch and of the Bible and continued to occupy me in my later development in painting and also in my iron work. Usually before I get into a larger work I make a great number of small sketches entirely free. That gives me a lot of freedom to use all the media I happen to find. Some of these encounters became major works. This piece of wood I developed until it was actually what I recognized to be the theme embedded in it.

VII

174

No. 70a
Mother and
Child

The traditional clinging of a child to the skirt of its mother is one of the most natural poses in the occurrences between the child and its mother. It shows the natural fear of the child in this world — seeking protection in the lap of its mother. The lap of the mother is actually the world of the child and without this protection its life would be unimaginable. The mother is proud to be the protector of her child and is the one who the child feels it can rely on, grasping her skirt which is the nearest thing.

Nos. 76 - 81
Moses Group

Iron, in our days, is not a material you can buy in an art store like any other art material. Those artists who need iron to work with have difficulties getting that material. Usually they rely on finding it in out-of-the-way places. That happened to me one day in the countryside when visiting friends in the vicinity of Cold Springs, N.Y. We passed an old blacksmith's shop and I entered trying to find some old pieces of iron. I saw there some large pieces of real iron, half rusted and decayed. For me this was a treasure. The appearance of the blacksmith was very forbidding and his words were very short. He asked me "What do you want?" I told him, "I need quite a few pieces of iron". He said, "I don't understand you. What do you mean — quite a few pieces?" I told him, "All the lot there" pointing to the big group of marvelous iron pieces standing together in front of a window. He said, "How will you take them?" I said, "I am with friends with a car — if you would like to sell them to me I'll be happy. We'll load them in the car and take them to my studio". "What for do you need such large pieces of iron in a studio?" he asked. "I am an iron worker", I said. "An iron worker?" He looked at me with suspicion, like a giant looking at a pygmy. "And what will I do without my iron?" I said, "I see that you didn't use this iron for a long time and the pieces you work on now are not from such iron. Now-a-days most of the blacksmiths don't use such iron anymore. It would be nice if you could sell me those pieces". When I told him that, he went to the open door, looked at our old jalopy and turned to me almost with pity — "You want to load this jalopy with that iron? Your jalopy will fly to heaven. You need some help". When I heard this and saw the way this giant had turned into a different person to whom one could talk I told him, "If you could find a day to deliver them I would be very thankful to you". He went over to the window, started to look at the marvelous pieces of iron while I went out to call my friends telling them, "Do you want to see something?" I called them in to see the group of iron the man might bring to me in the city. The blacksmith came over to us. He had become a different person. He said tersely, "If you want them you can have them. I hate to look at them — how they're standing there and I can't use them the way I used to. Where do you live?" I gave him my address. He said, "In three days I'll deliver the iron to you". As he had promised he delivered the iron three days later and he came punctually. He delivered those marvelous pieces of iron like a miracle. When I asked him "How much do I owe you for your iron and for the delivery?" he put up his hand like one who wants to get rid of something very disappointing and mentioned a sum that was like giving them away for nothing. He looked around at my strange pieces of sculpture and suddenly asked "Did you do that?" as if not able to believe what he saw. He was near the door already after I paid him and said "God bless you" and left quickly. From this group of iron I did all the six pieces of Moses which belong together.

No. 85
Alighting
Eagle

When I came to the Columbia River I saw two eagles alight and come to rest on one of the trees. I was excited by the tremendous dam there and the appearance of the salmon counting station. The unusual quiet of the power house inside and the sight of the two eagles alighting on a tree that was on a little island coming out from the depth of the mountains enchanted me so that I started to see a very strange landscape which reminded me of an old Chinese painting. Also this spot excited me because this was a place where Lewis and Clarke had passed through. All these unusual sights made me do the work on this eagle which I composed from pieces of iron I picked up on that little island.

No. 89
Apocalypse

This subject is a very common one in our time with all the terrible things going on in the world. I dwelt on this subject in my book REMEMBER which is on the holocaust.

No. 118
The Rabbi

The stone for this carving I found in my garden when we first moved into my new house in 1965. So I welcomed it to continue to stay in my garden as such a figure.

No. 127
A Legend
A Man Buys a
House I

A man buys a house. He moves into it. He feels at home in it. He works in it. He makes himself comfortable. He prays in it. He plants a garden around it.

No. 128
A Legend
A Man Buys a
House II

Another man buys a house. You don't see him sitting in it comfortably. He doesn't live in it or do any work in it. You don't see him putting flowers in his window or planting a garden around it. Just strange things you notice there. Finally one day you find him crushed under his house.

No. 132
Giant Owl

The Giant Owl is an owl I met in my youth when I walked through the Tatra Mountains in Poland. I met this tremendous creature late toward evening returning from an excursion near Morskie Oko, the well-known lake on top of a mountain. I was so frightened that I started to run. The creature seemed to be angry with me. I'll never forget that.

No. 134
Japanese
Dancers

The iron for these two dancers I found in iron mines near Cedar City in Utah which distinguishes itself historically as having the first iron mines in the country. We went out to look for those mines and found a number of marvelous abandoned pieces of iron with which we filled up our car. We couldn't send them home because they were too big and heavy to send by mail. We had to send them home by the railroad.

No. 136
Don Quixote
and Sancho
Panza

The theme of Don Quixote and Sancho Panza is universal which we can see in many cultures — the illusory approach to happenings in life.

VIII

Nos. 143,144
Celestial
Sphere
Celestial Face

These two pieces of iron, each one extremely interesting because of their quality and atmospheric character we found outside of Cedar City in Utah.

1. This Was A Shovel, Now It Is A Mask, 1975, Iron, 10½"
* 2. Praying Prophet, 1960, Iron, 12"
* 3. Variations On A Theme, 1963, Iron,   a 14"
                                                                   b. 17"
 c. 14½"
 d. 14"
 e. 13½"
4. Variations On A Theme, 1963, Iron, f. 12½"
 g. 14"
 h. 14"
 i. 13"
 j. 12"
5. Variations On A Theme, 1963, Iron, k.23"
 l. 16"
 m. 27"
 n. 19"
 o. 26"
6. Variations On A Theme, 1963, Iron, p. 11½"
 q. 12"
 r. 14"
 s. 14"
 t. 18"
* 7. Old Indian Head, 1975, Iron, 52"
* 8. Greek Dancer, 1969, Iron, 50"
9. Centaur, 1969, Iron, 29½", Alice and Henry Corning
* 10. Caterpillar, 1969, Iron, 16"
11. Wild Beast, 1978, Iron, 23"
12. Mechanical Tools, 1979, Iron, a. 9"
                                b. 11"
13. Acrobat, 1979, Iron, 28", The National Maritime Museum, Haifa
14. Ostrich, 1975, Iron, 24"
15. German Mythical Figure, 1970, Iron, 10"
     Prehistoric Skeleton, 1970, Iron, 10"
16. Rooster, 1969, Iron, 9½"
17. Fighting Warriors, 1970, Iron, 7"

* Indicates commentary by the artist.

18. Wasp, 1969, Iron, **35"** -
19. Bird Looking Back, 1976, Iron, 8"
    Angel, 1976, Iron, 8½"
    Owl, 1976, Iron, 6½"

20. Weasel, 1975, Iron, 6½"
    Man with Raised Arms, 1970, Iron, 8½"
    Twins, 1969, Iron, 6"
21. Figure I, 1978, Iron, 9"
    Figure II, 1978, Iron, 10½"
    African Bird, 1978, Iron, 10"
* 22. Beast, 1964, Iron, 13"
23. Mechanical Head, 1964, Iron, 14"
24. Dancer, 1971, Iron, 11½"
    Owl, 1971, Iron, 9"
    Figure, 1971, Iron, 8½"

25. Insect, 1969, Iron, 28", Alice and Henry Corning
26. Crowing Rooster, 1977, 27"
* 27. Cow, 1964, Iron, 9"
28. Eagle, 1975, Iron, 49"
29. Circus Manager, 1977, Iron, 23½"
*30. Man A Victim Of His Own Devices, 1977, Iron, 39", The National Maritime
Museum, Haifa

31. Rooster On A Fence, 1967, Iron, 19"
* 32. Masks, 1975, Iron, a. 12"
b. 11"
c. 14"
d. 13½"
e. 17"
f. 12½"
* 33. Strange Bird, 1977, Iron, 32½", Lillian and Joseph Miller
34. Whale, 1976, Iron, 18", The National Maritime Museum, Haifa
35. Praying Man, 1963, Iron, 28½"
36. Moses And The Falling Tablets, 1964, Iron, 27"
37. Enkidu, 1960, Wood, 17½"
38. Don Quixote, 1966, Iron, 12"
39. Praying Mantis I, 1966, Iron, 18"

40. Abstract Figure, 1966, Iron, 13½"

* 41. Poet Laureatus I, 1966, Wood, 20"
    Poet Laureatus II, 1966, Iron, 18"

42. Praying Mantis II, 1967, Iron, 62"

43. Minotaur, 1970, Iron, 51½", Alice and Henry Corning

44. Sacrifice Of Isaac, 1961, Iron, 54", The National Maritime Museum, Haifa

* 45. Jacob's Dream, 1975, Iron, 46"

46. Strange Birds, 1975, Iron,   a. 6½"
                                   b. 11½"
                                   c. 11½"
                                   d. 8"

47. Strange Birds, 1975, Iron,   e. 3¾"
                                   f. 4½"
                                   g. 4½"

48. Eagle On Its Nest, 1979, Iron, 20½"

49. Figure, Iron, 13½"

* 50. Moses, 1980, Wood, 25"

51. Head Of A Giant Bird, 1981, Stone, 9"

52. Masks, 1961, Iron, a. 9"
                           b. 10"
                           c. 8½"

53. Masks, 1973, Iron, a. 8"
                           b. 13"

54. Circus, 1973, Iron, 24"

55. Man On Stilts, 1982, Iron, 48"

56. Bathers In A Private Pool, 1981, Iron, 4½"

57. Demonstration, 1967, Iron, 18"

58. Masks, 1973, Iron, a. 7"
               1970   b. 14½"
                           c. 14½"

59. Father and Son, 1975, Iron, 13"

60. Little Figure, 1973, Iron, 6"
    Bird, 1973, Iron, 10"
    Owl, 1973, Iron, 12", Alice and Henry Corning
    Deer, 1973, Iron, 5½", Alice and Henry Corning
    Ostrich, 1973, Iron, 9"
    Little Woman, 1973, Iron, 6"

61. Bird On My Spiral Staircase, 1967, Iron, 17½"
62. Colosseum, 1975, Iron, 8"
63. Perplexed Bird, 1975, Iron, 20"
64. Coney Island Bather, 1970, Iron, 44"
65. Weight Lifter, 1969, Iron, 54"
66. Iron Masks, 1981, Iron, a. 9"
                                    b. 9"
                                    c. 12"
67. Fish, 1976, Iron, 9"
68. Bull, 1979, Iron, 19"
69. Young Girl, 1979, Iron, 29"
* 70. a. Mother And Child, 1979, Iron, 14"
        b. Woman Washing Hair, 1979, Iron, 13", Alice and Henry Corning
71. Bird Through A Window, 1981, Iron, 8", Alice and Henry Corning
      Bird Looking Back, 1981, Iron, 8½"
      Warrior, 1981, Iron, 13½"
      Bird With Long Beak, 1981, Iron, 8½"
72. Woman Riding Horse Side Saddle, 1975, Iron, 8½"
73. Ball Player, 1970, Iron, 17"
74. Incarcerated, 1964, Iron, 31", The National Maritime Museum, Haifa
75. Bishop, 1971, Iron, 54"
* 76. Moses Writing The Tablets, 1979, Iron, 24"
77. Moses On Top Of The Mountain, 1979, Iron, 30"
78. Moses Carrying The Tablets, 1979, Iron, 26½"
79. Moses Dropping The Tablets, 1979, Iron, 26½"
80. Moses Sees What Happened Below, 1979, Iron, 28"
81. Moses And The Dropping Tablets, 1979, Iron, 28"
81a. The Moses Group
82. David Playing On The Harp, 1965, Iron, 24", The National Maritime Museum, Haifa
83. Little Sea Monster, 1977, Iron, 16", The National Maritime Museum, Haifa
84. Peasant And His Wife, 1974, Iron, 10"
* 85. Alighting Eagle, 1965, Iron, 17", Private Collection
86. African King, 1965, Iron and Wood, 15", Private Collection
87. Quarreling Birds, 1971, Iron, 5"
88. Ruins Of A Temple, 1971, Iron, 7"
* 89. Apocalypse, 1975, Iron, 12", The National Maritime Museum, Haifa
90. Moses And The Tablets, 1975, Iron, 20", The National Maritime Museum, Haifa

91. Kohen Blessing Of The Priests, 1963, Iron
92. Little Kneeling Figure, 1973, Iron, 4½"
    Little Lamb, 1973, Iron, 4"
    Female Figure, 1973, Iron, 5"
93. Antique Figure, 1977, Iron, 23"
94. Exotic Bird, 1980, Iron, 11½"
    Acrobat, 1970, Iron, 27½" The National Maritime Museum, Haifa
    Confronting Bird, 1970, Iron, 10½"
95. Greek Sketch, 1965, Iron, 11"
96. Mask From An Old Forest, 1963, Wood, 12½"
97. Figure, 1979, Iron, 8"
98. Arguing Prophet, 1979, Iron, 17½"
99. Ancient Tyrant, 1979, Iron, 13½"
100. Warrior, 1970, Iron, 16"
101. Giant Bird, 1980, Iron, 22"
102. Canaanite Figures, 1981, Iron, 16"
103. Peaceful Birds, 1981, Iron, 17"
104. Dynamic Bird, 1981, Iron, 8"
105. Bird Preparing For Flight, 1981, Iron, 12½"
106. Alighting Bird, 1972, Iron, 9"
107. Bird In Flight, 1975, Iron, 12"
108. Diving Bird, 1962, Iron 13½"
109. Bird Looking Back, 1980, Iron, 5"
     Roman Figure, 1980, Iron, 4"
     Little Calf, 1980, Iron, 3"
110. Rooster, 1962, Copper, 24", Alice and Henry Corning
111. Strutting Bird, 1972, Iron, 3"
     Mexican Woman And Child, 1975, Iron, 3"
     Little Animal, 1975, Iron, 2½"
112. Weasel, 1962, Iron, 8"
113. Child With **Balloon, 1979, Iron, 19"**
     Figure, 1979, Iron, 14", Alice and Henry Corning
114. Preacher, 1979, Iron, 13"
     Reclining Figure, 1979, Iron, 4½"
     Singing Bird, 1979, Iron, 14½"
115. Pure Design, 1982, Iron, 12¾"
116. Sea Monster, 1982, Iron, 27"

117. Chanukah Menorah, 1962, Iron, 43″

*118. Rabbi, 1967, Stone, 37″

119. Primitive Head, 1970, Stone, 9″

120. Torso, 1962, Iron, 4″

121. The Chief, 1972, Iron, 11½″

122. Emerging Bud, 1962, Iron, 17″, The National Maritime Museum, Haifa

123. Rolling Horse, 1969, Iron, 6½″

124. Blessing Hands, 1963, Iron, 7½″

125. Fish Skeleton, 1962, Iron, 6″

126. Bull, 1962, Iron, 15″

*127. A Legend, A Man Buys A House I, 1977, Iron, a. 24″
                                                                             b. 9″
                                                                             c. 9½″
                                                                             d. 17″

*128. A Legend, A Man Buys A House II, 1977, Iron, a. 13″
                                                                             b. 15″
                                                                        c. 13″
                                                                              d. 8″

129. Old Age, 1963, Iron, 18″, The National Maritime Museum, Haifa

130. Man In Pursuit Of Success, 1967, Iron, 35″, National Maritime Museum, Haifa

131. Mexican Head, 1975, Iron, 16½″

*132. Giant Owl, 1978, Iron, 27½″

133. Fish And Waves, 1978, Iron, 12½″

*134. Japanese Dancers, 1981, Iron, 28½″, 39″

135. Girl In The Woods, 1981, Iron, 21″

*136. Don Quixote And Sancho Panza, 1963, Iron, 19″

137. Dancer, 1970, Iron, 12″

138. Bird Feeding, 1972, Iron, 6½″

139. Cow, 1972, Iron, 5½″

140. Bird In The Window, 1982, Iron, 7″

141. Chinese Lady, 1964, Iron, 7½″

142. Lizard, 1975, Iron, 6½″

*143. Celestial Sphere, 1978, Iron, 11½″

*144. Celestial Face, 1978, Iron, 8″

145. Hand Game, 1978, Iron, 7″

146. The End Of The Play, The Actors Bow, 1979, Iron, 5½″

Selected Data

EXHIBITIONS

1936	The Artists' Gallery	First One Man Exhibition
1936	Montross Gallery	The Ten
1936	Galerie Bonaparte, Paris	The Ten
1937	Montross Gallery	The Ten
1937	East River Gallery	Paintings and Drawings
1938	Georgett Passedoit Gallery	The Ten
1939	American Artist's Congress	Art in a Skyscraper
1939	Mercury Galleries	The Ten
1941	Bonestell Gallery	Paintings
1942	Bonestell Gallery	Paintings
1942	Bonestell Gallery	The Ten
1943	Buchholz Gallery (Curt Valentin)	Weather Vane Drawings
1943	Bonestell Gallery	Water Colors and Drawings
1944	The Institute of Modern Art, Boston	An Exhibition of Religious Art Today
1945	Bertha Schaefer Gallery	Paintings
1946	Bertha Schaefer Gallery	Paintings
1946	Bertha Schaefer Gallery	De Profundis Gouaches
1946	Taft Museum – Cincinnatti, Ohio	Paintings
1946	Office of Cultural Affairs, State Department	Group Exhibition
1947	Bertha Schaefer Gallery	Paintings
1947	University Museum of Art Ann Arbor, Michigan	Oils and Water Colors
1947	University of Iowa	Paintings
1947	Baltimore Museum of Art	Paintings
1948	The Art Institute of Chicago	Paintings
1948	Bertha Schaefer Gallery	Paintings
1948	Jewish Museum	Biblical Paintings
1950	Buchholz Gallery (Curt Valentin)	Biblical Themes 18 Etchings
1951	Bertha Schaefer Gallery	Paintings
1951	Buchholz Gallery (Curt Valentin)	Biblical Themes
1952	Jewish Museum	Biblical Paintings, Water Colors, Drawings
1953	Smithsonian Institution U.S. National Museum	Biblical Etchings

1955	Duveen-Graham	Paintings
1955	City Art Museum of St. Louis An Exhibition in honor of the Jewish Tercentenary in the United States	Biblical Paintings and Etchings
1956	Duveen-Graham	2nd & 3rd Portfolio of Biblical Etchings
1957	Bezalel National Museum, Jerusalem	Etchings on Biblical Themes
1957	Amerikanische Maler der Gegenwart — U.S. Committee of the International Association of Plastic Arts	Paintings — "Prophet on the Ruins"
1958	Peter H. Deitsch	Water Colors, Gouaches and Etchings
1959	Jewish Museum	A Retrospect — Paintings, Water-Colors, Drawings, Sculpture
1960	Yandes Gallery	Artists as Collectors, Artist's Works and Collections
1961	ACA Gallery	Paintings
1963	Minneapolis Institute of Arts	Contemporary and Ancient Art
1964	FAR Gallery	Etchings — Judges & Kings
1965	FAR Gallery	Drawings
1968	Klutznick Exhibit Hall, B'nai B'rith, Washington, D.C.	Exhibit of Paintings
1969	Brandeis University	Paintings and Etchings
1975	National Maritime Museum, Haifa	Paintings, Sculpture
1978	Haifa Museum	Paintings, Sculpture

BIBLIOGRAPHY

Articles about the artist
Catalogues, Journals, Magazines, Books

April 15, 1936, S.F.Z. Vol. 1, #10, cover photo with Ben-Zion drawing

April-June 1941 THE MENORAH JOURNAL, "A Live Year of Art", William Schack

April 1947, ART DIGEST, "Vigor of Ben-Zion", J.K.R. on Bertha Schaefer Show

December 1947, Baltimore Museum of Art news

March 1947, THE NEW YORKER, "A Matter of Taste", Review of exhibition at Bertha Schaefer Gallery

1947, THE NEW YORKER, "Jewish Museum Show", Robert M. Coates

1947, ADVANCING AMERICAN ART, U.S. Information Service, Prague, Hugo Weisgall

May 22, 1948, ART DIGEST, article by Alonzo Lansford

May 22, 1948, THE NEW YORKER, Review by Robert M. Coates

1948, CATALOGUE, Bertha Schaefer Gallery Exhibition, article by J. LeRoy Davidson

May 1948, CATALOGUE, Biblical Paintings at Jewish Museum, article by Stephen S. Kayser.

1948, NEW MASSES, "The American Painter", article by Joseph Solman

Summer, 1949, THE MENORAH JOURNAL, an album of paintings, drawings, and sculpture by 60 Jewish artists of America, Europe and Israel

1951, CATALOGUE, Exhibition, Amerikanische Maler der Gegenwart — D.S. Committee of the International Association of Plastic Arts — Ben-Zion painting "Prophet on the Ruins"

June 1, 1952, ART DIGEST, Cover reproduction, article by Dore Ashton

July-August, 1953, JEWISH LIFE, "Ben-Zion, Grandson of the Prophets", Alfred Werner

1952, CATALOGUE, Biblical Paintings, Jewish Museum, article by Stephen S. Kayser

May 24, 1952, THE NEW YORKER, Biblical Paintings at the Jewish Museum, review by Robert M. Coates

April 1953, IGAS (International Graphic Society), Stephen S. Kayser

1954, LE DESSIN CONTEMPORAIN AUX ETATS-UNIS, Musee National D'Art Moderne

1954, THE MODERN RENAISSANCE IN AMERICAN ART, Ralph M. Pearson, Harper Bros., N.Y. Pages 136-140

March 1956, PICTURES ON EXHIBIT "From the Editor's Notebook", Charles Z. Offin

January 1957, TEMPLE ISRAEL LIGHT, "Ben-Zion Creator of Biblical Art", Emery Grossman. Cover reproduction

1957, FIFTY CONTEMPORARY AMERICAN ARTISTS, Herman C. Gulack

October 1958, WORLD JEWRY, "The Art of Ben-Zion", Alfred Werner

September 17 - October 28, 1959, CATALOGUE, Jewish Museum, "Ben-Zion — A Retrospect", Stephen S. Kayser

October 3, 1959, THE NEW YORKER, The Art Galleries, Robert M. Coates

October 1959, ARTS — Month in Review, Sidney Tillim

1959, CONGRESS BI-WEEKLY, "Ben-Zion's Mighty Art", Alfred Werner

1960, CONGRESS BI-WEEKLY, "Ben-Zion and Ben Shahn", Alfred Werner

December 1960, THE RECONSTRUCTIONIST, Cover reproduction

December 30, 1960, THE RECONSTRUCTIONIST, Cover reproduction

January 13, 1961, THE RECONSTRUCTIONIST, Cover reproduction

January 27, 1961, THE RECONSTRUCTIONIST, Cover reproduction

April 1961, THE NEW YORKER, The Art Galleries, Robert M. Coates

1965, Artist's Proof #8, "On the Bible Etchings of Ben-Zion", Karl Schrag

1967, ART & TRADITION, Emery Grossman, Thomas Yoseloff Pub., Pages 31-38

1974, JEWISH AFFAIRS, "The Hebraic Vision of Ben-Zion, The American Jewish Painter", Alfred Werner

1976, THE JEWISH WEEK, AMERICAN EXAMINER, "The Thirty-Six Unknown", Sue Gardner

1980, AMERICAN PRINTS AND PRINTMAKERS, Una E. Johnson, Pages 112-115

1981, ANNUAL POETRY REVIEW, EKED, Tel Aviv, Israel, Yaffa Benyamini, Itamar Yaoz-Kest

PUBLICATIONS BY BEN-ZION

ART

1950	BIBLICAL THEMES, Curt Valentin, Portfolio of 18 etchings
1952	PROPHETS, Curt Valentin, Portfolio of 18 etchings
1954	THE BOOK OF RUTH, JOB, SONG OF SONGS, Curt Valentin, Portfolio of 18 etchings
1960	THE WISDOM OF THE FATHERS, The Limited Editions Club, Drawings by Ben-Zion
1960	ETCHINGS & POEMS; Morris Gallery, N.Y., Etchings of 21 artists for 21 poets
1964	JUDGES & KINGS, Graphophile Associates, N.Y., Portfolio of 18 etchings
1965	THE LIFE OF A PROPHET, Artist's Edition, Portfolio of 18 etchings
1966	THE EPIC OF GILGAMESH AND ENKIDU, Graphophile Associates, N.Y. 36 etchings
1967	IN SEARCH OF ONESELF, Artist's Edition, 14 self-portraits in drypoint
1975	THE 36 UNKNOWN, Artist's Edition, Portfolio of 36 etchings and poems
1980	THE 36 UNKNOWN, Eked, (English & Hebrew). Book based on portfolio of that name
1981	REMEMBER, Eked, Drawings and Paintings done during the holocaust years

POETRY (Hebrew)

1979	FROM THE SONGS OF BEN-ZION I, Eked (written 1919)
1980	FROM THE SONGS OF BEN-ZION II, Eked (written 1923)
1980	FROM THE SONGS OF BEN-ZION III, Eked (written 1923—1979)
1982	WALKS ON PATHS AND ROADS, Eked (written 1960—1978)
1983	IN THE BEGINNING (Epic poem), Eked
1983	FROM THE SONGS OF BEN-ZION V, Eked

DRAMA (Hebrew)

1921	THE STRUGGLES OF A VIOLIN, Nymin (Berlin)
1980	ADVERTISEMENT, Eked (Written 1930)
1980	KING SOLOMON, Eked (written 1919)
1981	THE STREET, Eked (written 1918)

BIOGRAPHICAL (Hebrew)

1980	IN THOSE DAYS, Eked
1983	IN THE PRIMEVAL FOREST, Eked

ESSAYS ON ART (English)

1963	''An Artist's View of a Jewish Museum,'' Article in the Jewish News
1982	REFLECTIONS ON SYMBOLISM AND THE ABSTRACT, Two Essays , Eked
1983	ON THE INNER LIFE, Eked

1/33

Ben-Zion

IX

In The Grip Of The Five Senses

Self Portrait from the portfolio of etchings IN SEARCH OF ONESELF

The approach to life and to art is very much bound up with the work of Ben-Zion. In bringing together his iron sculpture we have tried also to indicate its organic relationship to his poetry and his painting and to project the sculpture as an integral facet of his creative output. We have consciously avoided technical or psychological explanations and wherever possible we have endeavored to have the words of Ben-Zion himself come through.

The Editors

ACKNOWLEDGEMENTS

We would like to thank Stanley Lewis for his professional guidance and friendship, Ronald Gordon for his assistance with the design of the book, Kenneth Milford for his unfailing good humor, Geraldine Liphschutz for typing the manuscript and for her active participation. The translation of the poem ''The Stone in the Field'' from the Hebrew was done by Tabita Shalem. Photography credits are due Oliver Baker, Arik Baltinester, Geoffrey Clements, Eliot Elisofon, Sadeh Photos, Anja Valentin-Glazer, Todd Weinstein.

This first edition, BEN-ZION IRON SCULPTURE, is limited in number to five hundred copies. The printing of this book is by the MERIDEN GRAVURE COMPANY Meriden, Connecticut. The paper is Monadnock Dulcet. The book has been bound in Scholco Commodore Natuurlinnen by PUBLISHER'S BOOK BINDERY, Long Island City, New York.